Rat Terriers

Paige V. Polinsky

Checkerboard
Library

An Imprint of Abdo Publishing
abdopublishing.com

abdopublishing.com

Published by Abdo Publishing, a division of ABDO, PO Box 398166, Minneapolis, MN 55439. Copyright © 2017 by Abdo Consulting Group, Inc. International copyrights reserved in all countries. No part of this book may be reproduced in any form without written permission from the publisher. Checkerboard Library™ is a trademark and logo of Abdo Publishing.

Printed in the United States of America, North Mankato, Minnesota.
062016
092016

Cover Photo: iStockphoto
Interior Photos: iStockphoto, pp. 1, 5, 11, 19, 21; Shutterstock, pp. 7, 9, 13, 15, 17

Series Coordinator: Tamara L. Britton
Editor: Liz Salzmann
Production: Mighty Media, Inc.

Library of Congress Cataloging-in-Publication Data

Names: Polinsky, Paige V., author.
Title: Rat terriers / Paige V. Polinsky.
Description: Minneapolis, MN : Abdo Publishing, a division of ABDO, [2017] |
    Series: Dogs set 13 | Includes index.
Identifiers: LCCN 2016007738 (print) | LCCN 2016012843 (ebook) | ISBN
    9781680781786 (print) | ISBN 9781680775631 (ebook)
Subjects: LCSH: Rat terrier--Juvenile literature.
Classification: LCC SF429.R35 P65 2016 (print) | LCC SF429.R35 (ebook) | DDC
    636.755--dc23
LC record available at http://lccn.loc.gov/2016007738

Contents

The Dog Family 4

Rat Terriers 6

What They're Like 8

Coat and Color 10

Size 12

Care 14

Feeding 16

Things They Need 18

Puppies 20

Glossary 22

Websites 23

Index 24

The Dog Family

Dogs are one of the most popular pets of all time. In fact, there are more than 100 million pet dogs worldwide! And they are all part of the family **Canidae**. Coyotes, foxes, and wolves also belong to this family. Scientists believe that dogs **evolved** from gray wolves.

Thousands of years ago, the first **domesticated** dogs helped humans hunt. They also helped fight off danger. Dogs later guarded property, herded livestock, and pulled carts and plows. Many still do today!

Over time, dogs were **bred** for specific qualities and uses. There are now more than 400 dog breeds worldwide. The rat terrier, or ratty, is one of them. This smart, spunky dog is an expert **exterminator**. It is also a wonderful family pet!

The rat terrier makes an intelligent, loving companion.

Rat Terriers

The rat terrier has been called a "**breed** of many breeds." Its English ancestor, the feist, was a mix of many different terriers. The feist was used for hunting and rat baiting in the early 1800s. Its speed and strong jaws made it an excellent rat catcher.

People started bringing feists to the United States in the 1850s. It became a popular farm dog. It helped hunt, guard property, and catch **vermin**.

Breeders began crossing the feist with other dogs to improve its abilities. They bred it with the whippet, greyhound, and beagle. This improved the breed's sight, speed, and scenting ability. They also bred the feist with the Chihuahua, toy fox terrier, and toy Manchester terrier. This produced a smaller breed.

This new breed was a tiny powerhouse. Theodore Roosevelt, US president in the early 1900s, had one.

One rat terrier killed more than 2,500 rats in 7 hours!

He called his dog a "rat terrier" because it cleared the White House of rats. And the name stuck! In 2013, the **American Kennel Club (AKC)** recognized the rat terrier as an official **breed**.

What They're Like

Don't be fooled by the rat terrier's size. This little pup has a huge personality! The ratty is playful, active, and up for anything. Even though this **breed** is full of energy, it's calmer than most other terriers. It is friendly and curious about the world around it.

However, this breed is territorial and suspicious of strangers. This makes it an excellent watchdog. And the rat terrier has a strong prey drive. It does not do well with smaller animals.

The rat terrier forms a strong bond with its owner. It is very loyal and sensitive to its owner's moods. The ratty is also a rewarding dog to train because it is very intelligent. With the right motivation, a rat terrier can learn many commands.

A ratty can get along
with animals it lives
with. But it is often
wary of strange animals.

Coat and Color

The rat terrier has a short, **dense**, and smooth coat. The **breed** comes in many colors, including blue, **lemon**, and chocolate. Most ratties have at least a little bit of white fur. The most common ratty coloring is black, white, and tan.

The ratty's coat also comes in different patterns. Piebald ratties are white with **random** spots of color. Other rat terriers have a large blanket-back marking that cover their back and tail. Many ratties have a mask of color around their eyes.

No matter the color, these dogs **shed** a moderate amount. Regular weekly brushing will reduce shedding. But each spring and fall, the ratty loses more fur than usual. It needs extra brushing during this time.

The AKC recognizes 18 official color combinations for the rat terrier.

Size

Standard ratties are 13 to 18 inches (33 to 46 cm) tall. They weigh between 12 and 25 pounds (5.4 and 11 kg). **Miniature** rat terriers are only 10 to 13 inches (25 to 33 cm) tall. They weigh 10 to 16 pounds (4.5 to 7 kg). There are also larger Decker ratties and tiny toy ratties. But the **AKC** only recognizes the standard and miniature sizes.

The ratty is meant to have an athletic, **flexible** build. This **breed** has strong hindquarters, small paws, and straight, slender legs. It also has a long, tapering tail. But breeders often dock the tail short.

This compact breed has a smooth, wedge-shaped head. It often has an alert, intelligent expression on its thin face. The ratty's large ears are usually pointed. Its eyes are wide-set and oval shaped. A ratty's eyes can be a variety of colors, from amber to gray.

Ratties of all sizes
love to snuggle
up in bed.

Care

The rat terrier is generally a solid, healthy **breed**. But it does have certain health risks, similar to any other dog. Small breeds such as the ratty are more likely to have knee problems. The rat terrier is also at risk for allergies and crooked teeth.

Keep your ratty healthy by scheduling regular checkups. Your veterinarian can test your dog's vision and hearing. The vet can also give your dog important **vaccinations** and **spay** or **neuter** it.

Grooming your rat terrier will help it feel its best. Keep your dog's teeth clean by brushing them frequently. This will also give your ratty healthy gums and fresh breath! Be sure to trim your dog's nails every couple of months. And check its ears weekly for any sign of infection.

You should always
be gentle with the
ratty's delicate legs.

Feeding

The rat terrier's abundant energy depends on a quality diet. There are many wet, dry, and semi-moist foods available. Your ratty's food should be rich in protein and healthy fats. But its specific **nutritional** needs depend on its age, size, and activity level. Work with your vet to determine the best plan for your ratty.

Your puppy should generally eat three meals each day. After all, it's still growing! Feed your puppy the same food that it ate at the **breeder**'s. Your adult ratty will only need about two meals a day. Make any food changes gradually to help your dog adjust. And always have fresh water available.

Be careful not to overfeed your rat terrier! An overweight ratty is at risk for **obesity**. This can lead to heart disease, **diabetes**, and other health problems.

Being overweight is especially hard on the ratty's sensitive joints. A fit, healthy ratty will live a longer, happier life.

Schedule regular mealtimes to help manage your ratty's weight.

Things They Need

The rat terrier's jumping and digging skills make it a true escape artist. So a high fence and watchful eye are **essential**. Your ratty will also need basic supplies. This includes a leash, collar, and identification tags. Food and water dishes are also necessary.

This smart, energetic **breed** gets bored easily. So physical and mental exercise is key for your ratty's well-being. Activities such as jogging or **agility** training will help prevent destructive behavior. Your ratty will also appreciate some challenging toys. This terrier loves trying to solve a good puzzle!

A roomy crate will give your ratty a comfortable place to rest. It will also make **housebreaking** easier. But love and attention are just as important as supplies. The social ratty gets **separation anxiety** more easily than other **breeds**. So it will need plenty of quality time with you!

The ratty often becomes attached to certain toys and blankets.

Puppies

A mother rat terrier is **pregnant** for 63 days. She then gives birth to a **litter** of four to seven puppies. At first, these pups cannot see or hear. Their ears stand straight up.

After two weeks, a ratty's ears and eyes start working. Ratty puppies receive their first **vaccinations** at six weeks old. At eight weeks, they are ready for their new homes!

Take your time when picking out a rat terrier. Visit your local shelter or choose a responsible **breeder**. Spend time with the ratty before making a decision. Ask a lot of questions about its health and personality.

You can begin training your new rat terrier immediately. Puppy kindergarten classes are a great way to train and **socialize** your ratty. Be kind and patient with your pup as it adjusts. Introduce it to new people and places. With love and care, your playful rat terrier will live 13 to 15 years!

Some rat terrier puppies' ears flop over and others' ears stick up.

Glossary

agility - a sport in which a handler leads a dog through an obstacle course during a timed race.

American Kennel Club (AKC) - an organization that studies and promotes interest in purebred dogs.

breed - a group of animals sharing the same ancestors and appearance. A breeder is a person who raises animals. Raising animals is often called breeding them.

Canidae (KAN-uh-dee) - the scientific Latin name for the dog family. Members of this family are called canids. They include wolves, jackals, foxes, coyotes, and domestic dogs.

dense - thick or compact.

diabetes - a disease in which the body cannot properly absorb normal amounts of sugar and starch.

domesticated - adapted to life with humans.

essential - very important or necessary.

evolve - to develop gradually.

exterminator - someone who gets rid of something completely.

flexible - able to bend or move easily.

housebreak - to teach a dog to not go to the bathroom inside.

lemon - a shade of tan that is so light it appears to be yellow.

litter - all of the puppies born at one time to a mother dog.

miniature - a copy of something in a reduced size.

neuter (NOO-tuhr) - to remove a male animal's reproductive glands.

nutritional - related to that which promotes growth, provides energy, repairs body tissues, and maintains life.

obesity - the condition of having too much body fat.

pregnant - having one or more babies growing within the body.

random - lacking a definite plan or pattern.

separation anxiety - a strong feeling of fear and worry when not with one's caregiver.

shed - to cast off hair, feathers, skin, or other coverings or parts by a natural process.

socialize - to adapt an animal to behaving properly around people or other animals in various settings.

spay - to remove a female animal's reproductive organs.

vaccination - a shot given to prevent illness or disease.

vermin - small harmful or unwanted animals, such as fleas or rats.

Websites

To learn more about Dogs, visit **booklinks.abdopublishing.com**. These links are routinely monitored and updated to provide the most current information available.

Index

A

American Kennel Club 7, 12

B

body 10, 12, 14, 16, 17
breeder 6, 12, 16, 20

C

Canidae (family) 4
character 4, 8, 16, 18, 19, 20, 21
coat 10
collar 18
color 10, 12
crate 18

E

ears 12, 14, 20
energy 8, 16, 18
exercise 18
eyes 10, 12, 20

F

food 16, 18

G

grooming 10, 14
guarding 4, 6

H

head 12
health 14, 16, 17, 18, 20
herding 4
history 4, 6, 7
hunting 4, 6, 7

L

leash 18
legs 12, 14
life span 17, 21
litter 20

N

nails 14
neuter 14

P

paws 12
puppies 16, 20, 21

R

reproduction 20
Roosevelt, Theodore 6, 7

S

senses 6, 14, 20
shedding 10
size 6, 8, 12, 14, 16
socialization 20, 21
spay 14
speed 6

T

tail 10, 12
teeth 14
training 8, 18, 20

U

United States 6

V

vaccinations 14, 20
veterinarian 14, 16

W

water 16, 18
White House 7